Glorious Agony

Written By: Hannah French

Illustrated By: Eliza Laurie French

Copyright

Acknowledgement

To my daughter Eliza, thank you for illustrating my book beautifully; for sharing your creativity with me, and for believing in mine.

To Nathan, thank you for your constant patience, support and enthusiasm throughout the editing and publishing process.

Dedication

To my girls, my world.

May you always trust the Light that has overcome the darkness.

Author Testimony.

Let the redeemed of the Lord say so, whom He has redeemed from the hand of the enemy. (Psalm 107:2)

Growing up in the church as the daughter of vicar meant I always had a knowledge and mindfulness of God. I am deeply thankful to my parents for providing me with this spiritual foundation. Even so, I did not understand the Man at the centre of my Bible stories. I failed to grasp that God came to earth as Jesus Christ to grant me access to Himself, and that He created me with purpose (Ephesians 2:10 & 18). I did not comprehend that Satan existed as a genuine adversary who would relentlessly seek to destroy me (1 Peter 5:8). Yet to appreciate these biblical truths, the Lord remained mysterious. We designated Sunday for worship, and prayer served as a bedtime ritual rather than a lifestyle. My small measure of faith didn't have a huge impact on me day-to-day.

My parents divorced during my pre-school years, so my normality involved having a weekday home and a weekend home. Though both loving, these surroundings contrasted in terms of structure and parenting, causing confusion. School I found to be a distressing and often hostile environment that added to my uncertainty about the world and my place within it. Despite my quiet nature, I longed for friendship, but struggled to establish or maintain the connections that came effortlessly to others. Detached and lonely, reading became a solace as books provided other worlds in which to escape. As my vocabulary expanded, I began writing; diaries developing into poems and songs. I enjoyed using words to express my feelings, which seemed rather deep and sensitive when compared to my carefree peers.

The alienation I experienced increased as I continued through secondary school, and I sought ways to form relationships. From a young age, I had discovered that smoking and drinking provided comfort and fun for adults, and now engaged in these habits myself. Alcohol's influence felt like a superpower. It dampened intrusive thoughts and enabled me to become a social creature. My party trick of tolerating dangerous amounts of liquor seemed to make me popular. My sober self was someone I neither understood nor liked, so the mask of drink and drugs became my life and personality, and I fell away from the church community.

With no confidence to function in the real world, I wasted my academic ability and opportunities to find my passion and purpose, spending my college years with other outcasts. These friendships were still meaningful to me because people accepted and desired my company; something I rarely experienced in childhood. Nevertheless, the harsh truth of the superficiality of my relationships hit when I became pregnant at nineteen. The end of my party days left me without the support of my partner or my 'friends'. Despite this, having a baby inside of me thrilled me. Engrossed in books about pregnancy and fascinated by the stages of infancy, I was excited to nurture my very own child. Seeking comfort, I revisited the Bible and gazed up at the God who answered prayer, still with little understanding of my professed faith or genuine connection to the One I hoped would guide me. I continued to escape into classic literature, naming my firstborn after the heroine of Austen's 'Pride and Prejudice'. My life was a curious contradiction between naive idealism and a sinful, unstable reality. Holding intrinsic traditional values, whilst committed to a detrimental relationship that inwardly made me despair, I returned to alcohol to calm the overwhelm, becoming dependent.

During my second pregnancy in this relationship, I joined a newly built church in my neighbourhood, enthusiastic about raising my children within a godly community. It was here that I learned God is not an addition to the Christian life; He *is* life. Faith is not a ritual, but a personal relationship with Jesus Christ. My baptism followed, as well as repeated attempts to quit drinking. Meanwhile, my partner was sinking deeper into serious drug addiction and severe mental illness. The relationship ended for good and I endured a period of debilitating anxiety, suffering ongoing episodes.

Although now supported by authentic friendship and love from my family in Christ, I was unaware of my prolonged state of dysregulation and inability to make healthy decisions. Another destructive relationship followed, which quickly became a marriage. I still attended church on Sundays as a member of the worship team. Using my voice to praise the Lord and serving Him in the community was a pleasure so different from drinking. It gave me a taste of the peace and contentment I craved. I wanted these pure activities to consume my life, and to rid myself of the shame of hidden sin. To the outside world, I appeared to function well, my children being my focus and my joy. However, I did not recognise the poor quality of life we had because of my codependency. I survived on happy moments with my daughters, in an otherwise sad existence. Throughout it all, I spent a significant amount of time in God's Word and prayed regularly. It sometimes felt pointless and certainly hypocritical, yet I knew the scriptures contained words of life and truth and they gave me hope. I completed a medical detox to rid myself of drink for good. It worked for a time, but a much deeper work needed completing in my spirit, so it wasn't effective long term. Powerless; alcohol addiction tormented me for over 10 years.

My third daughter arrived, and once again I felt delighted, and still determined to create a large and loving family. Unfortunately, the more I understood the gospel and desired wholeness, allowing Jesus into my life to heal and restore, the more I experienced isolation and antagonism in my marriage. We moved away from family, and shortly after, I suffered a bereavement. Anxiety consumed me to the degree that I was afraid to be awake and afraid to be asleep. Under these circumstances, I found it hard to walk into a new church, but it soon became a sanctuary, as home felt more and more unsafe. The care and companionship I received there helped me to cope, but life was hard. The pastor invited me to lead worship and my spirit soared at the prospect, but the contradiction I was living was taking its toll. It took one night of unbearable conviction to change the course of my life. Some old friends invited me for a drink, but I couldn't enjoy myself. Serving God whilst living in darkness weighed too heavily upon me. Unable to think of anything else, I had to stop. Conscious of my weakness, I looked to the Lord for help to make this my last drink. After attending church, reading the Bible and praying for years, I understood who Jesus was and why He came; to save, and His gracious Holy Spirit now urged me to be rescued. Tired enough of life my way, I agreed with Him wholeheartedly. This decision meant experiencing a time of near unbearable suffering that I endured by abiding in the Lord's presence. He sustained me as I stayed sober in the combative atmosphere I called home. Determined not to sin, I constantly cried out to the Lord for strength. Hour by hour, I put one foot in front of the other.

On waking one morning about a month later, I rose with a new sensation. Despite the unfamiliarity of it, I knew what had occurred, and hesitated to accept it; I was free. God heard every prayer sent up over the years, the feeble ones I mustered for myself and the prayers of faithful believers burdened for me. Jesus saw every tear of anguish, having compassion on my complete brokenness before Him and dependence on His promises. Some credited me with the willpower to overcome, but only God's power could remove the desire. That was a miracle, and I now understood that 'if the Son makes you free, you shall be free indeed' (John 8:36). All the unrelenting thoughts were gone; I experienced no temptation. Jesus had broken the chains of addiction. I cried and laughed and sang. My praises felt unbound and heaven open to receive them. Writing and singing worship songs became my favourite pastime.

As I grew closer to God, the enemy continued to attack and my marriage deteriorated further. I was now living in an unpredictable environment with increasing violent tendencies being shown by my husband. When the threat of violence turned towards me, I fled the family home with my girls. We lived in my sister's dining room for half a year as she helped me to function with the terror that lived in my heart. Every night I spent in the Bible, crying out to God. He carried me through the hardest time of my life and led me towards a better way, providing strength, and a new home in safe, rural surroundings. Acquiring a newfound appreciation for nature, the beauty of God's creation enveloped me as a simple and wholesome lifestyle brought therapeutic tranquillity. The Lord had shown me in His Word during the awful months before I left home, to 'sit at His feet and learn from Him' (Luke 10:39). I have done so ever since.

An arduous journey of healing began. Being diagnosed with trauma and OCD required long-term therapy. Having support from a domestic violence charity meant learning that both of my relationships were abusive. This was incredibly tough to face, but necessary to process and recover from. Later, I also discovered I was autistic, which has helped me to understand my lifelong confusion, reframe the past, and accept the person I am; the one I despised for being different. I now embrace the unique soul that God granted me, and function on the firm foundation of His Word, grounding and directing me. The truth of scripture has brought me into the way of peace, countering my previous distress in a world I failed to navigate. And I now live with the hope of a better world to come, that places ongoing challenges into perspective. I look forward to the day I am raised incorruptible (1 Corinthians 15:52), which holds more meaning now that I also live with acute, chronic pain. This has been a major obstacle, physically, mentally, and emotionally. However, the periods of rest in Jesus dictated by disability have taught me more about His steadfast love and deepened my relationship with Him.

My little family still carries burdens of suffering because of our troubled past. But God is always active, and I trust Him for continued restoration that will glorify His name. The consequences of my sin live on, but the guilt and shame need not. I am forgiven, and a new creation in Christ with a hope and a future (2 Corinthians 5:17). Satan persists to oppress and disturb, but I now abide in the shadow of the Almighty (Psalm 91:1). I am assured I will live eternally with my Saviour, so anxiety no longer consumes or has the power to deceive me (Hebrews 2:14 & 15). Though my body has weakened, God strengthens my Spirit (Ephesians 3:16). I look forward to the day He returns to establish a new heaven and earth, where there will be no sorrow, no sin, no devil, and no death. (Revelation 21:1 & 4).

I will forever thank the Lord for His mercy, forgiveness, transforming power, and future hope. This is the good news of the gospel of Jesus Christ that has the power to save. It isn't only addicts who need salvation, 'for all have sinned and fall short of the glory of God.' (Romans 3:23) We are all in need of a Saviour who grants life everlasting, 'for the wages of sin is death, but the gift of God is eternal life in Christ Jesus our Lord.' (Romans 6:23)

We will never be free from tribulation until we are free from sin, but having the Spirit of the living God dwelling within is having a love that never forsakes and a foretaste of heaven, and we are to share this hope with others here and now.

God created us for His pleasure (Revelation 4:11). It is in pleasing Him we find our own deep satisfaction. We have a commandment to love Him and to love one another (Matthew 22:37-40), and using our individual gifts for this purpose is the way to our own fulfilment. God has blessed me with a passion for creativity, and a heart to praise His name. I love to write poetry and sing songs that would encourage others to seek His face and to know His love.

Table of Contents

Preface

Writing creatively has always been the way I have journaled through life. Now that my poetry declares the faithfulness of God, it is being shared as a witness to the fact, and hopefully as an encouragement to others.

Glorious Agony was produced in the wilderness and the valley. I have learned to value moments of hardship and solitude as opportunities to strengthen my relationship with Jesus; leaning on Him, receiving from Him, and growing in Him. The Lord's promises are treasures that may lie undiscovered during times of ease. Though affliction is never desirable, it is inevitable. And the child of God can take heart, Jesus is always working all things for the good of those who love Him (Romans 8:28). It is in the darkness we earnestly seek and appreciate the Light of the world (John 8:12), who desires to draw near and conform us to His image (Romans 8:29).

Christ's suffering made it possible for us to be restored to God (Colossians 1:20). Through His resurrection, we have the confident assurance of an eternity without sorrow (1 Corinthians 15:20). Trial may mark our lives, but with Jesus, we can see the glory in the agony.

For I consider that our present sufferings are not worthy to be compared with the glory which shall be revealed in us.

(Romans 8:18)

Glorious Agony

Now the Son of Man is glorified, and God is glorified in Him.
(John 13:31)

How could it be, Majesty?
You would take the blame for me
Undo my shame, my heart to clean
By faith, free indeed

On bended knee, I receive
Your sacrifice, my liberty
How could it be Majesty?
Glorious agony

How could it be, Majesty?
You would shape Gethsemane
Hands that created the tree
Impaled for my release

On bended knee, I receive
Your sacrifice, my liberty
How could it be Majesty?
Glorious agony

How could it be, Majesty?
You call me to blood-stained feet
Life-giving wounds I sit beneath
Meeting every need

On bended knee, I receive
Your sacrifice, my liberty
How could it be Majesty?
Glorious agony.

Offering of Praise

Therefore by Him let us continually offer the sacrifice of praise to God, that is, the fruit of our lips, giving thanks to His name (Hebrews 13:15)

Why would praise be an offering of sacrifice?

It recognises grace when God hides His face

It sees goodness in the darkness

When growing faith is tested

And the enemy suggests we are forsaken

Praise honours Sovereignty

While we are trampled all around

And taste the suffering of the Son

Melted down, there In the heat

Worship will rise as incense sweet

Building a wall around our lonely frame

Through which no poison fog can permeate

Praise reiterates we are created

In the image of Messiah

It reminds of our refining to His likeness

That we are cared for by the Father

Every hair on our head in His Hand

And the trusting of His plan

Praise is truth brought into focus

It was never about us

Through pain or glory

He is worthy of our praise.

We Do Not Sorrow

I do not want you to be ignorant, brethren, concerning those who have fallen asleep, lest you sorrow as others who have no hope. For if we believe that Jesus died and rose again, even so God will bring with Him those who sleep in Jesus.
(1 Thessalonians 4:13 & 14)

We do not sorrow as those with no hope
No tear cried out falls to the ground
Each drop of anguish, the Lord collecting
To turn the enemy around

We do not sorrow as those with no hope
Despite the blows life has rained down
Though battle weary, each scar for Jesus
Endured with joy, becomes a crown

We do not sorrow as those with no hope
Jesus carries our every grief
Sin and burden, He gladly lifts from saints
Bowing before His pierced feet

We do not sorrow as those with no hope
A comfort for us who remain -
Precious ones asleep in Jesus will rise
To greet us on that joyful day

We do not sorrow as those with no hope
We're passing through this desert land
We'll cross the river to sing forever -
'Holy and worthy is the Lamb!'

Rise and Thrive

And he prayed that he might die, and said, "It is enough! Now, Lord, take my life"…suddenly an angel touched him, and said to him, "Arise and eat."
(1 Kings 19:4b & 5)

In desperate loneliness, I cry -

'I cannot strive, but lie here and die'

A delicate whisper passes by -

'Eat this bread, rise and thrive,

Do not weary, do good, my child.'

His quiet breath of life revives

My emptiness for strength divine

Once more I cry, with hope this time -

'My Lord, please live this life of mine.'

Hannah French

Richer Blood

Knowing that you were not redeemed with corruptible things, like silver or gold…but with the precious blood of Christ.
(1 Peter 1:18 & 19)

I cannot purge or take away
The sin that flows within my veins
Temptation rife, how could I stand?
After each fall, covered in shame

I cannot cleanse or purify
A heart inclined to be defiled
No dirty work would satisfy
No deed achieves eternal life

To richer blood You would point me
Blood that was drawn so viciously
Became ingrained in Calvary's tree
Oh richest blood, stain me!

I cannot love You Lord, in truth
Without Your covenant anew
No zeal or sorrow I produce
Could tear the temple veil in two

I cannot claim that I possess
One thing of worth or righteousness
You died so that I would find rest
You rose that I'd know holiness

To richer blood You would point me
Blood that was drawn so viciously
Became ingrained in Calvary's tree
Oh richest blood, stain me!

Count the Cost

*Whoever does not bear his cross and come after Me cannot be
My disciple. For which of you, intending to build a tower, does
not sit down first and count the cost.*
(Luke 14:27 & 28)

Are you building on the Rock
Who saved you by His blood?
Does the ground beneath your feet
Hold fast despite the flood?
Are you tearing down the walls
Made with a heart of stone?
Declaring, 'Jesus Christ is now my home!'

Count the cost, are you picking up your cross?
Are you living for the One who sacrificed?
Count the cost, are you prepared to suffer loss?
And together with the Lord, be glorified!

Is the castle of your pride
In ruins at your feet?
Are the shame and the defeat
Bringing you to your knees?
Are you mourning over sin?
You will be comforted
The Lord, will be your fortress and your guide!

Count the cost, are you picking up your cross?
Are you living for the One who sacrificed?
Count the cost, are you prepared to suffer loss?
And together with the Lord, be glorified!

Do you dare to stand alone
On earth, our battleground?
When your friends call it home

11

And the enemy surrounds
Are you holding up God's Word
Your only shield and sword?
Stand firm until you hear the trumpet sound!

Count the cost, are you picking up your cross?
Are you living for the One who sacrificed?
Count the cost, are you prepared to suffer loss?
And together with the Lord, be glorified!

Follow and Obey

My sheep hear my voice, and I know them, and they follow Me.
(John 10:27)

The world and its toys
The crowd and the noise
Are making us stray far from home
A purpose we hold
Not silver or gold
To love Jesus, who makes us whole

He laid down His life
He made a today
Let Him show the way
He gave you His life
He gave you today
Follow and obey

The crowd and the noise
The world and its toys
Are drowning out His gentle voice
He's calling us home
From the busy road
There's peace within the Shepherd's fold

He laid down His life
He made a today
Let Him show the way
He gave you His life
He gave you today
Follow and obey.

Living Stone

Behold, I lay in Zion a chief cornerstone, elect, precious, and he who believes on Him will by no means be put to shame.
(1 Peter 2:6)

My Rock
The One on which I stand
In the storm
That would overwhelm
Merely shapes the clefts
Where I dwell
Living Stone
Build me up in You
My only hope
My only home

This Rock
On which I now depend
Though struck with rage
Scars remaining
Water pours forth
Life sustaining
Living Stone
Build me up in You
My only hope
My only home

One Rock
Rejected cornerstone
On which some stumble
Others stand
Ageless mountain
Unshaped by hands
Living Stone
Build me up in You
My only hope
My only home.

Fountain of Life

For with You is the fountain of life.
(Psalm 36:9)

Fountain of water

Fountain of blood

How I am rescued by a great flood!

Cleansed from my sin

And pulled from the grave

Fountain of life poured out to save!

The Strength of the Lord

The Lord will give strength to His people; The Lord will bless His people with peace.
(Psalm 29:11)

When rising tides would overtake
Winds tear away peace
When I fail and flail
And fear a fall into the deep
Yet underneath are Hands
That stilled the seas
The strength of the Lord
Holds and comforts me

When I seem to have no sight -
Wilderness to valley
When my fearful heart
Would fill my mind with unbelief
Yet the darkness flees
When the truth I seek
The strength of the Lord
Clears the way for me

When I would forsake Your way
And glory in my strength
When I speak with foolish pride
Trust only in myself
Yet empty hands
Are all I have to bring
The strength of the Lord
Restores me again.

Once Far Off

*But now in Christ Jesus you who once were far off have been
brought near by the blood of Christ.
(Ephesians 2:13)*

Once far off, now brought near by the blood
Once in fear, danger on every side
Once astray, with darkness my only guide
Now resting in the shadow of I Am
The Lion is my Shepherd through the Lamb

Once far off, now brought near by the blood
Once without hope, a stranger to God's voice
Once only death, the grave my only choice
Now raised to life, in heaven I sit with Him
The King is now my Father through the Son

Once far off, now brought near by the blood
Once enslaved, now I am a child of God
Once deceived, now I am no longer lost
The wall broken down, the veil torn in two
Once far off, now brought near by the blood.

A Good Name

A good name is to be chosen rather than great riches, loving favour rather than silver and gold.
(Proverbs 22:1)

A name that brings glory to Your name
Is all I want to hold
A name that brings glory to Your name
Worth more to me than gold
Worth more than precious, fragrant oil
Is Your abiding presence
A name that brings glory to Your name
Is all I want to hold

A name that brings glory to Your name
Is all I want to hold
A name that brings glory to Your name
Worth more to me than gold
Worth more than earthly honour
Is to bring You heavenly praise
A name that brings glory to Your name
Is all I want to hold

A name that brings glory to Your name
Is all I want to hold
A name that brings glory to Your name
Worth more to me than gold
Worth more than might or power
Is to reign with You forever
A name that brings glory to Your name
Is all I want to hold.

Free is the Slave of Christ

But now having been set free from sin, and having become slaves of God, you have your fruit to holiness, and the end, everlasting life.
(Romans 6:22)

Free is the slave of Christ
Dying to know abundant life
Bound to the One who bonds untied
To leave the old man in the grave
Dust of the earth passing away
My portion forever to be
Jesus eternally

Free is the slave of Christ
A home prepared with God on High
His Spirit comforts and abides
Covered in His perfect goodness
One day to be pure and blameless
My heart now a throne for Jesus
To dwell eternally

Free is the slave of Christ
Serving the One who gave His life
Perfect humility and might
Sin and death are now broken chains
By love that leaves no life the same
My soul no longer held by fear
Redeemed eternally.

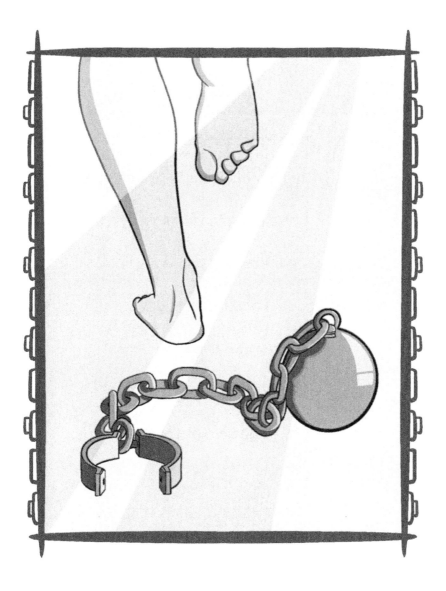

That Day

Looking for the blessed hope and glorious appearing of our great God and Saviour Jesus Christ.
(Titus 2:13)

Lord, I look to that day

There I am whole before Your throne

No disturbance or decay

There Your worship is my home

Lord, until that day

There is weeping and lament

In the dust I live and receive

There at the hem of Your garment.

Who is This Man?

Who can this be, that even the winds and the sea obey Him?
(Matthew 8:27)

They followed Him into a boat
On Galilee serene
As Jesus slept, they thought
On all His wondrous words and deeds
Will our teacher become king?
No one spoke or healed like Him
Surely our lives will never be the same!
Who is this man? Who can this be?
A voice divine, heavenly authority
Lepers are cleansed, lame rise to their feet
He Promises life for all who believe!

The waves that gently lapped the boat
Began to rock so fierce
The breeze became a mighty wind
Bringing them to their knees
In a moment, their world was filling
With chaos and fear -
'Master, save us, or we all perish here!'
Who is this man? Who can this be?
The storm we now face does not threaten His peace
How can He rest while we fight for our lives?
If we can wake Him, we might survive!

Jesus rose and as He spoke
The waters stilled, the sky calmed
Nature bowed before His voice
And His mighty, outstretched arm
He is the Prince of peace

He is the Rock on which we stand
Where is our faith? This is the Great I Am!
Who is this man? Who can this be?
He is to be feared far more than these seas
The earth hears His voice, obeys His command
Surely He holds the world in His hand!

Your Heart

I will give you a new heart and put a new spirit within you; I will take the heart of stone out of your flesh and give you a heart of flesh.
(Ezekiel 36:26)

Walls around stone
Crumbled
Stumbled upon truth
Looking
Outside for blame
Residing
Within tears
Calling
From the fall
Drying
Amongst dying embers
Covering
A face on the ground
Hoping
For fire
Consuming
This shell
Filling
A will with treasure
Given
To the Life-Giver
Returned
A heart burned and buried
Beating
With new life.

The Glory of God

For there is born to you this day in the city of David a Saviour, who is Christ the Lord. And this will be the sign to you: You will find a Babe wrapped in swaddling clothes, lying in a manger. (Luke 2:11 & 12)

A light dawned in the darkness
After many silent years
Bethlehem shone as a virgin's Son
Was born into poverty
While she laid Him
In a manger quietly
Herod and his city trembled
At the prophecy

The Glory of God
Wrapped in swaddling cloth
Far from palace and dignity
Causing heavenly host to light up the sky
Declaring His Majesty

Wise men, knowing they had found
The bright and morning star
Cared only that they follow Him
Not for the journey far
As they bowed to worship
Beneath the guiding light
Inside the crib, they were to find it
The Way, the Truth, the Life

The Glory of God
Wrapped in swaddling cloth
Far from palace and dignity
Causing heavenly host to light up the sky
Declaring his Majesty

Despised and weary shepherds
Ran with joy to find
The One of whom the Angel spoke
Hearts ablaze, as Judah's skies
Awestruck when they saw Him -
Like a Lamb upon the straw
Jesus Christ the Lord
Today a Saviour has been born!

The Glory of God
Wrapped in swaddling cloth
Far from palace and dignity
Causing heavenly host to light up the sky
Declaring His Majesty.

Home

He has clothed me with the garments of salvation, He has
covered me with the robe of righteousness.
(Isaiah 61:10b)

In Wilderness
I found a friend
Called loneliness
Who took me
From dry wells
Of no relief
That could not fill
Or clothe
A broken vessel
With no home

In Sanctuary
I found a throne
To sit beneath
A scarlet river
Flowed
For my relief
That cleansed
And covered me
In a robe so clean
And led me home.

What Can Be

*Behold what manner of love the Father has bestowed on us, that
we should be called children of God!
(1 John 3:1)*

A sheep off course can be found in time

A dying branch can find life within the vine

A worm can feed from the richest soil

A wretch can touch the hem of a garment unspoiled

A broken foundation can form a spring

A woman at the well can be a daughter of the King

A thirsty heart can be quenched by grace

A lamp uncovered can start a furnace

A wounded hand can heal another

The Son of God can become my Brother.

The Burden

*Come to Me, all you who labour and are heavily laden, and I will
give you rest. Take My yoke upon you and learn from Me, for I
am gentle and lowly in heart, and you will find rest for your souls.
For My yoke is easy and My burden is light.*
(Matthew 11:28-30)

The burden
Lies in wait
To crush a heart
With its weight
Look outside the gate
Up to the tree
Not within
There lifted high
The only Way
For it to fall
And make alive
Thirst for living rivers
To never die
Only to sin
His word within
A new heart
Burns to bring
The burdened
To the mercy seat
To be relieved
Lay your cares down
At the cross
Where gain is the loss
Hold to the prize
Heaven waits
Through narrow gates
All joy within
A crown
To cast before the King.

Seasons

To everything there is a season, a time for every purpose under heaven.
(Ecclesiastes 3:1)

Seeds of sorrow sown
In the season of our tears
Sheaves of gladness reap
When the time for harvest nears

To churn the soil is painful
Weeds that pierce and choke
Pulling up and cutting back
All that hinders growth

The shoot draws from the root
The source of its power
Giving branches to the vine
Fruit to the flower

Beaten by the storm
The sapling learns its duty
To become a life divine
Strength precedes beauty

Rain must fall and fall
Prepare this earthly garden
Weathered trees stand tall
Fit for a heavenly kingdom

The Light appears to clear
Heavy clouds of mourning
Revealing paradise
A new season dawning.

36

Years to Hear

The world is passing away…but he who does the will of God
abides forever.
(1 John 2:17)

Most of the years
Given to me
Spent unable to see
The waste of yesterday
Never to be replaced
Or taken back
The rest of my years
Given into Your hands
Now I understand
Today is a chance
To live my life for You
I give it back
All of our years
You prepare mansions fair
No tomorrow disturbs
A heart lost to the world
Waiting for You
To come back.

Glory to God in the Highest

*God, who at various times and in various ways spoke in time
past to the fathers by the prophets, has in these last days
spoken to us by His Son.
(Hebrews 1:1 & 2a)*

Let all the angels of God worship Him
The Father has spoken through His Son
Though He lies on a bed of straw
His throne is forevermore

Glory to God in the highest!
For peace and light and eternal life
Glory to God in the highest!
The mercy of God delivered at night
In Jesus Christ

Let all the angels of God worship Him
The Maker of heavens has come down
Though He cries to be cradled now
One day every knee shall bow

Glory to God in the highest!
For peace and light and eternal life
Glory to God in the highest!
The mercy of God delivered at night
In Jesus Christ

Let all the angels of God worship Him,
The Father gave us His only Son
Though He dies before growing old
Death is finished through His own

Glory to God in the highest!
For peace and light and eternal life
Glory to God in the highest!
The mercy of God delivered at night
In Jesus Christ.

Desire

Do not labour for the food which perishes...I am the bread of life.
He who comes to me shall never hunger.
(John 6:27a & 35a)

Desire for comfort
Desire for ease
Truth undesired
Diluted belief
Aggressive desire
The self to please
Feeds an insatiable enemy

Hungry for Jesus
Desire to heal
Truth desired
Restored belief
Spirit-filled
Abiding peace
Bread of life meeting every need.

By Faith

*But now they desire a better, that is, a heavenly country.
Therefore God is not ashamed to be called their God, for He has
prepared a city for them.
(Hebrews 11:16)*

By faith, we dwell in a foreign land
In tents made by Almighty hands
We live as strangers on the earth
'Til Jesus calls us home

Wanderers with the promise
Children of God, never lost or alone
Raised to life and abiding in Christ
His kingdom forever our home

By faith, we hope for a better land -
Heavens made by Almighty hands
We set our minds on things above
'Til Jesus calls us home

Wanderers with the promise
Children of God, never lost or alone
Raised to life and abiding in Christ
His kingdom forever our home

By faith, until the end, we stand
The world removed by Almighty hands
The sky rolled up, the stars all fall
When Jesus calls us home

Wanderers with the promise
Children of God, never lost or alone
Raised to life and abiding in Christ
His kingdom forever our home.

43

The Great I Am

Jesus said to them, "Most assuredly, I say to you, before
Abraham was, I AM".
(John 8:58)

Before the world was formed
You are The Great I Am
Every life unborn
Fashioned by your Hand
Creator and Sustainer
Alpha and Omega
You were, You are, You'll always be
The Great I Am

Before Abraham was
You are The Great I Am
Through every changing age
Your Word unaltered stands
Creator and Sustainer
Alpha and Omega
You were, You are, You'll always be
The Great I Am

Ancient of Days
You made a way
By faith, your children walked
Into the promised land
Today, the same
Your grace, the way
We come into your kingdom
By the blood of the Lamb
Redeemer and Saviour
Faithful and forever
Then and now, eternally
The Great I Am

Before The Great I am
Every knee will bow
And every eye will see
Your glory in the clouds
Creator and Sustainer
Alpha and Omega
You were, You are, You'll always be
The Great I Am.

My Shepherd

The Lord is my Shepherd; I shall not want. (Psalm 23:1)

Pastures green
Waters still
Staff will keep me from the edge
Shepherd true
Rod protects
In the darkness, lamps are lit
Shadows fall
Table set
Shame awaits the enemy
Fragrance sweet
Oil is poured
Mercy, goodness, never leave
Head is covered
Heart restored
Cup so full it overflows
Life abundant
Home awaits -
To dwell with You forevermore.

Heartleap

*My flesh and my heart fail; But God is the strength of my heart
and my portion forever.
(Psalm 73:26)*

The heart

Beats to believe

Feels to seek

Longs to meet

Who it needs

To be

He safely keeps

The last beat

From fear

The heart

Leaps in eternity.

The Rescue

*We went through fire and through water; But You brought us out
to rich fulfilment.
(Psalm 66:12b)*

Conforming closeness
Otherwise unknown
I would not have you leave
For a life of ease
Though through fire
Refining
Though through flood
Cleansing
Though alone
Never alone
Redeeming rescue
Otherwise unknown
I would rather be carried
Than deny I fell
Take me bruised across the river.

Are You There God?

I will never leave you nor forsake you.
(Hebrews 13:5b)

Are You there God?
It's dark and I'm scared
I thought I had studied
Believed I was prepared
I knew about trials
That temptation would come
Prepared to face troubles
One by one
But they're fierce and constant
And raging relentless
I'm not supposed to despair
Or depend on my senses
I'm hoping some roots
Hold this battered frame
Please tell me Your book
Still bears my name
Then I can bear this storm so rough
That would tear from me
All that I've heard of Your love
It would shake and disturb
So no peace can reside
It would rip up foundations
Do I really abide?
It's dark and I'm scared
That Your presence has gone
All I have are the pages
Your Spirit breathed on

Who told me to trust
Even when I can't see
That You will never leave nor forsake me
Please come and find me
I've lost my way
I never wanted to wander
I don't want to stray
Help me, Lord, in my unbelief
May the light of Your truth
Make the darkness flee
I'm reading the words
But fear and shame
Battle with the faith I claim
I seek Your will
But the strength I can't find
The power to live
It was never mine
Wasted pain
Time after time
May my heart, now exposed
Be renewed and refined?
As the sun rises
So Your mercy persists
As the world is held
So in You I exist
You are there God
Help me understand
That I'm safe
And engraved in the palm of Your hand.

The Way

Jesus said… "I am the way, the truth, and the life."
(John 14:6a)

I want to be held
By scarred hands
That know pain

I want to be led
By pierced feet
To know The Way.

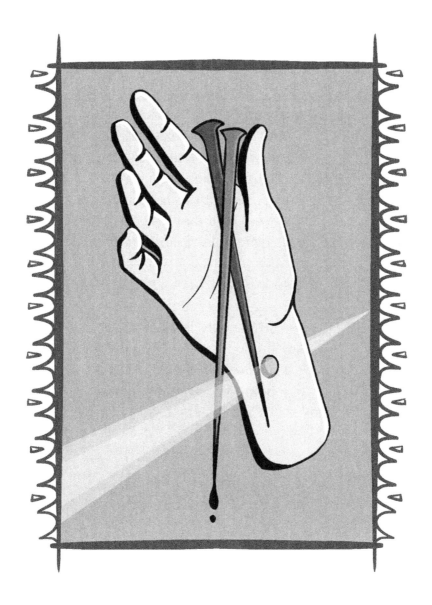

55

Praise the Lord

*Make a joyful shout to the Lord, all you lands! Serve the Lord
with gladness; Come before His presence with singing.
(Psalm 100:1 & 2)*

Praise the Lord with every breath
His mercy has extended
Praise the Lord with every step
His perfect light is guiding
Praise Him with your life anew
With everything that He gave you
Make a joyful noise before His throne

Praise the Lord, in heaven adored
The angels worship - 'Holy!'
Praise the Lord in all the earth
His church declares Him worthy
Praise Him with thankful voices
Love poured into hearts rejoicing
Make a joyful noise before His throne.

Myrrh in the Air

They presented gifts to Him: gold, frankincense, and myrrh.
(Matthew 2:11b)

There was myrrh in the air
When the giver of life
On a borrowed bed lay sleeping
Lifted up from the straw
To His mother's full heart
Where thoughts of Him she was keeping
'Do not be afraid'
Was the angel's refrain -
'Of His kingdom there will be no end'

There was myrrh in the air
When the giver of life
On a wooden cross lay bleeding
Lifted glorified eyes
To the Father on high
With love and prophecy keeping
The disciples were afraid
Yet to contemplate
The wounds designed for their healing

There was myrrh in the air
When the giver of life
From a borrowed tomb came breathing
Mary lifted her head
To a voice she knew well
Asking her why she was weeping
'Do not be afraid'

The angel had said -
'Not the dead, but the living you're seeking'.

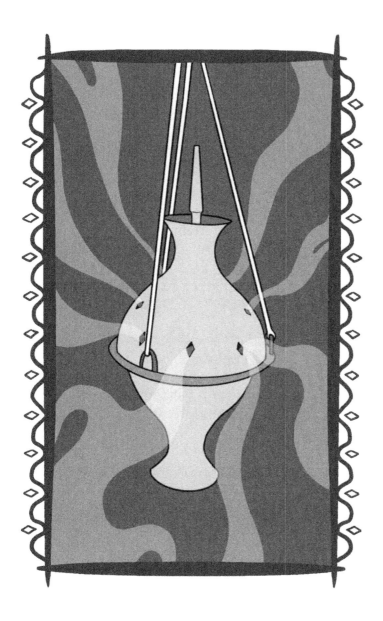

Mercy

Have mercy upon me, O God, according to Your lovingkindness;
According to the multitude of Your tender mercies, blot out my
transgressions. Wash me thoroughly from my iniquity, and
cleanse me from my sin.
(Psalm 51:1 & 2))

My sin is ever before me
Lord have mercy
My sin is ever before me
Father, hear my plea -
Wash me, cleanse me
With your holy fire
Create beauty from these ashes
From the dust, revive

Your grace is ever before me
As I approach your throne
Your grace is ever before me
A stray child welcomed home
How to thank You
For love ever outpoured
And sin removed from east to west
May I ever adore.

Oh Happy Certainty!

Who shall separate us from the love of Christ?
(Romans 8:35a)

Oh, happy certainty!
That peace with God has brought to me
Wounded hands reach out to heal
All who would receive
Hands that once were bound
To set the captives free!

Oh, hope blessed and sure!
That promises a better home
Thankful hands reach out to praise
In New Jerusalem
Uncorrupted hands
That worship God alone!

Oh, happy certainty!
Of heavenly security
Everlasting, mighty arms
Forever underneath
Nothing can ever take
God's love away from me!

First to Thirst

Whoever drinks of the water that I shall give him will never thirst.
But the water that I shall give him will become in him a fountain
of water springing up into everlasting life.
(John 4:14)

First to thirst
Reaching
From within
To be filled
And satisfied
By wells
Outside ourselves
Driven
By anxious longing
Distracting
From every thought
The source
Earnestly sought
Not to be bought
Or wrought
From broken cisterns
Deceiving
Turning interest
Into earnest need
Life-Giving Stream
Says 'Come to Me'
Searching ends
Upon receiving
Endless springs
Quenching

Eternal blessing
From the Fountainhead
Who made us
First to thirst.

Love

We love Him because He first loved us.
(1 John 4:19)

Love condescended to think upon me
Reach into darkness and misery
Love that was more than I could bear
Persisted when It couldn't be felt

Love I considered only torment
Became my source of joy and strength
Love so pure it was my shame
Tenderly covered and rid of blame

Love that took my blindfold away
The only light that could penetrate
Love that dared to lay all exposed
Shone on crooked paths and shadows

Love that lifted a guilty head
Redirected wayward steps
Love that taught me how to trust
A deeper love than dust to dust

Love poured out of a heart well fed
To comfort others who fell and despaired
Love, even here had the victory
I love because You first loved me.

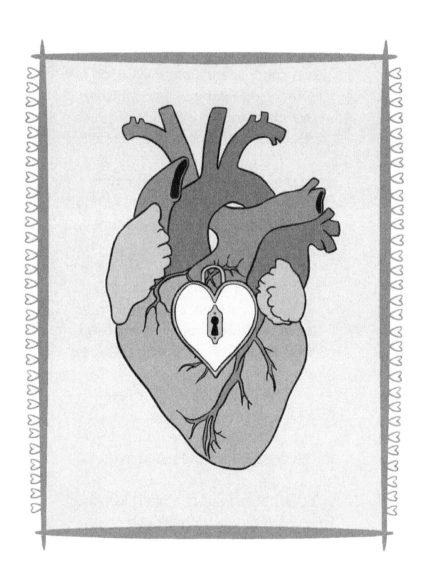

Heaven

To know the love of Christ which passes knowledge; that you may be filled with all the fullness of God.
(Ephesians 3:19)

Undisturbed by distraction
Untainted by corruption
Unstained by transgression
Unhindered by confession
Hearts that function
With full comprehension
Of the depth of love
That came from heaven.

Death To Life

Therefore if the Son makes you free, you shall be free indeed.
(John 8:36)

I looked upon a sparkle
Breathing in a pleasant wave
Its power such, a swirl enough
To take me to its taste
Beneath the swirl a current
That would bring me to my knees
A sparkle that would blind
On glistening waves
That rode the darkest seas

I looked upon a tree
That grew to lure me
Beneath the grape, a snake
Lying in wait among the leaves
A bite that would sedate
With a sting that came too late
Poison strong
Hope almost gone
As venom flowed through my veins

The bittersweetness of wine
Entangled in the vine
Fruit that brought pleasure
Violent and quick
Left stains upon my soul

I looked upon an empty cup
That once assured the cure

Elusive still, only fulfilled one promise -
Thirst for more
Shackled hands would shake
The cup again to take
A tightening grip
with every sip
Drowning in a flood I poured

The bittersweetness of wine
Entangled in the vine
Fruit that brought pleasure
Violent and quick
Left stains upon my soul

I looked upon a Man
Who drank a bitter cup for me
Hands that nails held to the tree
Released a scarlet river clean
That poured into the mire
Restored my sight
And set me on my feet
I looked for light
And I saw Calvary

I look upon a Love
That runs so deep it lifted from the grave
A heart that is forever free
To sing and never crave
Your sacrifice
Brought me from death to life
I thirst no more
A wellspring overflows
And satisfies

Your love is sweeter than wine
Abiding in the Vine
Living water
Bringing forth fruit -
Joy within my soul.

71

About the Author

Hannah was born in Salisbury, raised in the city of Swansea, and now lives in Carmarthenshire, along the river Tywi. She has largely been a stay-at-home mother to her three beautiful daughters.

Hannah considers faith and family to be the most important aspects of her life, and as a born-again Christian, her passion is to write and sing as an act of worship, and as a witness to the goodness of God.

When Hannah isn't writing she may be found at the beach with her Cavachon, who shares her appreciation of nature. Hannah loves the simple life and finds pleasure in literature, music, crafting and company. She believes almost every activity can be enhanced by a good cup of tea.

Glorious Agony is Hannah's first poetry book, inspired by her journey through faith.

Printed in Great Britain
by Amazon

45068313R00050